The Young Scientist Investigates

Sea and Seashore

by
Terry Jennings

 CHILDRENS PRESS ®

CHICAGO

Illustrated by
Karen Daws
Ann Winterbotham
Map by Rudolph Britto

Library of Congress Cataloging-in-Publication Data

Jennings, Terry J.
    Sea and seashore / by Terry Jennings.
       p.   cm. — (The Young scientist investigates)
    Originally published: Oxford : Oxford University Press, 1981.
    Includes index.
    Summary: An introduction to the animal life of the sea and
seashore. Includes study questions, activities, and experiments.
    ISBN 0-516-08441-0
    1. Marine biology—Juvenile literature. 2. Seashore biology—
Juvenile literature. [1. Marine animals. 2. Seashore biology.]
I. Title. II. Series: Jennings, Terry J. Young scientist investigates.
QH95.7.J46   1989
591.5'2636—dc 19   89-454
                                                         CIP
                                                         AC

North American edition published in 1989 by
Childrens Press®, Inc.

© Terry Jennings 1982
First published 1982 by Oxford University Press

Printed in the United States of America
1 2 3 4 5 6 7 8 9 10 R 98 97 96 95 94 93 92 91 90 89

The Young Scientist Investigates

Sea and Seashore

Contents

The Sea

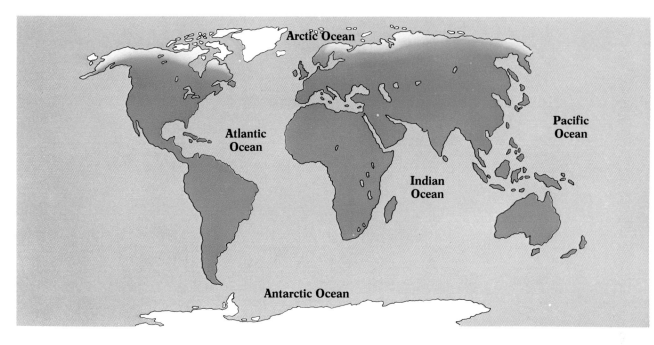

If you look at a globe or a map of the world, you will see that there is much more water than land. Nearly three-quarters of the world is covered by water. There are five great oceans and a number of smaller seas.

Seawater is always salty. The salt has come from some of the rocks the sea has covered. Warm seas are much saltier than cold ones. The Red Sea is very salty. But the saltiest sea in the world is the Dead Sea. The Dead Sea is so salty that no plants or animals can live in it. If people swim in the Dead Sea the salt in the water keeps them from sinking.

We usually think of the sea as being blue. But seawater is really colorless. The sea looks blue because it reflects the sky. The sea reflects the sky just as a mirror reflects anything held near it. On dull, cloudy days the sea looks gray.

Above: the sea under a blue sky

Below: the sea under a gray sky

The seashore and sea bottom

Where the land meets the sea is called the shore. Not all seashores are sandy. Some are rocky. Some are muddy. Some shores are covered with small stones called shingle. Others are covered with larger stones called pebbles or with big lumps of rock called boulders. Some seashores have high cliffs behind them.

Sandy shore

Many people think that the bottom of the sea is flat like the seashore. But it is not flat at all. There are high mountains under the sea, just as there are on land. There are deep valleys too. There are even big volcanoes. Some small islands are the tops of high mountains under the sea. Tall islands in deep water are usually made of rock from volcanoes at the bottom of the sea.

Some parts of the sea are so deep that the sun's light can never reach them. Here it is always darker than the darkest night.

Rocky shore

Mountains and valleys under the sea

4

Tides and waves

High tide

Low tide

The sea is never still. Tides and waves keep the sea moving. Twice each day the level of the water in the sea rises. The sea covers the shore. Waves may crash against the rocks and cliffs. We say that the tide is in.

Twice each day the level of the sea falls. The seashore and seaweeds are uncovered. We say that the tide has gone out. The tide is said to flow as it comes in, and to ebb as it goes out. As the tide is turning there is a short period when the water does not seem to move much. This quiet time is known as slack water.

Tides can be very useful to man. High tide brings deep water to harbors and ports. Sailors and fishermen can sail in and out of ports and harbors with the tide. Sometimes tides are dangerous. A very high tide can cause flooding.

Waves are caused by the wind. A wave goes on growing until its top turns over and breaks. Big waves can batter down rocks or wear away a cliff. They can tear down buildings and lift huge pieces of rock. Sailors have sometimes seen waves 50 feet high.

Formation of waves

Backwash of previous wave

Breaking wave

Peaking wave

Crest

Trough

Shore

Sea bed

Plankton and whales

Lots of animals and plants live in the sea. Millions of tiny plants and animals called plankton live near the top of the sea. Many plankton plants and animals are so small that you cannot see them. They can be seen only with a microscope. The tiny plankton plants use sunlight to make food.

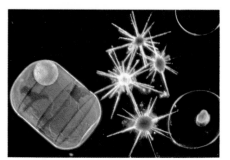

Plankton as seen under a microscope

As we have seen, the sea usually looks blue or gray. Sometimes the sea is brown, green or red. This is because of the plankton. There may be so many little plankton plants and animals in the sea that they color it.

The plankton plants and animals are eaten by larger animals. The fish we eat live on plankton. Many big whales also feed on the tiny plankton animals. The blue whale is the biggest animal that has ever lived. It may be over 100 feet long and weigh more than 150 tons. A blue whale feeds on tiny plankton animals. It often eats 2 tons of plankton in a day.

Herring feeding on plankton

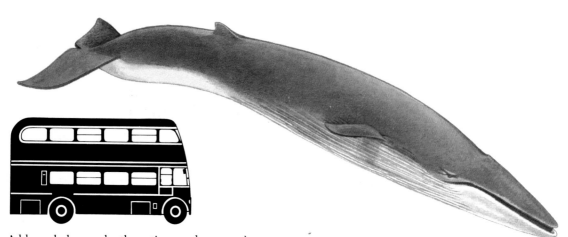
A blue whale may be three times as long as a bus.

Mollusks

Mussel

Cockle

Flat periwinkle

Dog whelk

Limpet

The seashore is the home of many creatures that are related to the slugs and snails on land. They are called mollusks. Mollusks have soft bodies and are often protected by a hard shell. Some mollusks, such as cockles and mussels, have two shells fitting closely together.

One common mollusk is the periwinkle. There are several different kinds of periwinkle. They all look rather like snails. But each has a little lid over the entrance to the shell. Periwinkles live on wet rocks, breakwaters and pieces of seaweed. When a periwinkle is underwater, it moves the little lid from the mouth of its shell and crawls along like a snail. Periwinkles eat pieces of seaweed.

Rough periwinkle   Common periwinkle

Rather similar to the periwinkle is the dog whelk. But the dog whelk shell has a different shaped opening. Dog whelks can be several different colors. They feed on barnacles.

Another common mollusk is the limpet. When the tide is out the limpet clings tightly to a rock using its yellow sucker. When the tide comes in, the limpet moves over the rocks eating tiny green seaweeds. As the tide goes out again, the limpet returns to exactly the same spot. There is often a groove in the rock where each limpet lives. The groove has been made by the limpet's shell.

7

Some more seashore animals

Barnacles look a little like mollusks. But they are really relatives of crabs, prawns and shrimps. Barnacles have hard pieces of shell around their bodies. Often there are hundreds of barnacles together on a rock. They feed on plankton when the tide is in. The barnacles scoop up the plankton with their feathery legs, which come out of the top of the shell.

Barnacles

Sea anemones are common in rock pools. Although they look like flowers, sea anemones are really animals. Sea anemones move very little and spend most of the time fixed to the same piece of rock. At the top of the sea anemone's body is its mouth. Around the mouth is a ring of long tentacles. They are used for catching small sea creatures. When the tide is out, or if the anemone is attacked, it can draw its tentacles into the body.

Beadlet anemone feeding on shrimp

A relation of the sea anemone is the jellyfish. The body of a jellyfish is shaped like an umbrella. The jellyfish swims by opening and shutting the umbrella. Underneath the umbrella is a mouth with long tentacles around the edge. These tentacles have stingers on them that are used to kill the jellyfish's food. Some jellyfish are very large. Their tentacles may be up to 100 feet long. The sting of a really big jellyfish is dangerous.

Common jellyfish

Portuguese man-of-war

Sandy beaches

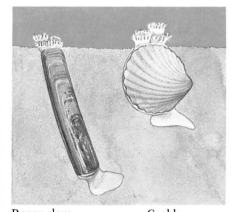

Razor clam   Cockle

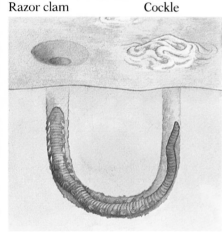

Lugworm

If you walk along a beach when the tide is out, few living things can be seen. But there are animals in the sand. Cockles live just below the surface of the sand. Razor clams live a little deeper down. Both cockles and razor clams are mollusks. They have two shells hinged together. Cockles and razor clams put out little tubes from their shells when the tide is in. They suck in sea water and get bits of food from it.

Often in the wet sand or mud you can find lugworm casts. The lugworms live in burrows that are shaped like the letter U. Each lugworm swallows sand or mud and gets little pieces of food out of it. The rest of the sand or mud is sent out of the other end of the hole and forms the cast. You can usually see a little hollow where the lugworm has sucked in mud or sand. Lugworms can be 10 inches long. Fishermen use them as bait.

Sometimes on the beach you can find little tubes in the sand that are about the size of a pencil. The tubes are made of grains of sand stuck together. Sand worms live in these tubes. Feather-duster worms also live in tubes made of sand.

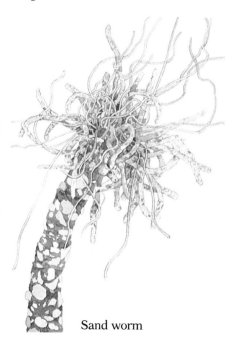

Sand worm

Feather-duster worm

Rock pools

When the tide goes out, some animals are left in the pools. Others hide under the rocks. This way they stay damp until the tide returns.

Most fishes leave with the tide but blennies hide under the rocks. Pipefish hide in rock pools. They are like small eels. The male pipefish carries the eggs that the female has laid.

Crabs are also often found under rocks and in pools. Crabs have five pairs of legs. One pair of legs has pincers at the end. Crabs walk sideways. One common crab is the hermit crab. A hermit crab has no shell of its own. It uses an empty seashell to live in. As the hermit crab grows bigger it has to find a larger shell.

Prawns and shrimps are relatives of crabs. Prawns are often found in rock pools. Shrimps live in the sand at the bottom of rock pools.

All of these animals have to stay where they are until the tide comes in. If they dry out they quickly die. This is why it is important that if you turn stones over on the shore to look for things, you put the stones back exactly as you found them.

Mussels

Saw wrack

Sea lettuce

Shrimp

Anemones

Bladder
wrack

Blenny

Edible crab

Pipefish

mit crab

Prawn

Barnacles

Hermit crab
(in whelk shell)

Razor
clam
shell

Starfish and sea urchins

The starfish is a common animal in rock pools. It is often found washed up on the shore. The starfish has arms that spread outward from the body. It is shaped like a star. Most starfish have five arms. But some have more. Underneath the starfish's arms are hundred of tiny tube feet. They are used for walking over rocks.

Starfish feed on oysters and mussels. They can be a pest to fishermen. In days gone by, fishermen used to tear in half any starfish they caught. The broken starfish were thrown back into the water. But the fishermen did not know that two new starfish could grow from the two halves.

Common starfish

Common sunstar

Starfish growing new limbs

Tube feet of starfish

The sea urchins that live on some parts of our shores are related to starfish. They too have hundreds of tiny tube feet. But they do not have the long arms. Sea urchins move slowly on their spines and their tube feet. Their feet enable them to walk up steep rocks.

Sea urchins feed on seaweed. They eat the seaweed using the five teeth they have sticking out of their undersides. The empty shells of sea urchins are often sold in shops at the seaside for use as ornaments.

Common sea urchin from above

from below

Tube feet of sea urchin

Do you remember?

(Look for the answers in the part of the book you have just been reading if you do not know them.)

1 How much of the world is covered by water?

2 Which is the saltiest sea in the world?

3 Why does the sea look blue?

4 What do we call the place where the land meets the sea?

5 What is the bottom of the sea like?

6 How many times a day does the tide come in?

7 What are waves caused by?

8 What is plankton?

9 What animals feed on plankton?

10 What is the biggest animal that has ever lived?

11 How may pairs of legs does a crab have?

12 Where does the hermit crab live?

13 Name three relatives of crabs.

14 How many arms do most starfish have?

15 How do starfish and sea urchins move along?

16 What happened to the starfish fishermen used to tear in half?

17 What do we call the family of animals to which cockles, mussels, limpets and periwinkles belong?

18 How do barnacles catch their food?

19 How do sea anemones catch their food?

20 How does a jellyfish move?

21 What does the jellyfish use its stinger for?

22 How many shells do cockles and mussels have?

23 How do cockles and razor clams get their food?

24 What is the lugworm's burrow like?

25 What is the sandworm's home like?

Things to do

1 **Mark coastal towns and cities on a map of the United States.** Trace a map of the United States into your notebook. Mark on it where you live. How far do you live from the Pacific Ocean? How far do you live from the Atlantic Ocean?

2   Try to find a hermit crab. Gently tip its shell over. Watch carefully to see how it turns itself over again and walks away.

3   Try to find a starfish. Place it on the sand or rock underwater in a pool. Watch it move along. If you pick the starfish up carefully, you will be able to see the tiny tube feet moving backwards and forwards on its underside.

4   Use graph paper to make a map of a rock pool. Show where the different kinds of seaweeds grow. Make a list of all the kinds of animals you can find in the rock pool.

Take a small piece of raw meat or fish and feed some of the animals in the rock pool. Place the piece of meat or fish on the bottom of the pool. Watch quietly to see what kinds of animals come out to feed.

5   Make a collection of empty seashells. Clean them in tap water and brush off any sand or mud with a soft brush. Dry the shells and store them in shoebox lids lined with cotton. The shells will last forever in the box. Label each shell with its name and where and when you found it.

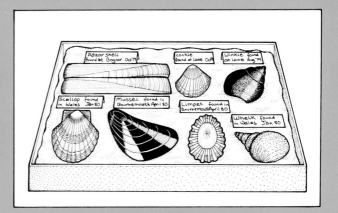

6   Use seashells to make necklaces and bracelets or a collage. Carefully make small holes in some empty seashells using a sharp nail. Thread the shells to make necklaces and bracelets.

Draw a large picture on a sheet of paper. Then glue seashells onto the picture to make a collage.

Seaweeds	Animals in Pool
A Sea lettuce	Crabs
B Grass kelp	Shrimps
C Sea moss	Cockles
D Channel wrack	Limpets
E Sea bett	Periwinkles
F Peacock's tail	Dog whelks
G Pod weed	Anemones
H Irish moss	
I Red laver	

15

7   Decorate some small boxes, flowerpots or picture frames with seashells. To do this you will need some plaster of Paris or one of the powdered substances used to fill cracks in walls.

Put a little of the powder into a jam jar. Add a small amount of water and stir thoroughly. Keep adding water a little at a time until you have made a thick paste. Smear the paste thickly all around the outside of the box, flowerpot or picture frame. Gently push seashells into the paste while it is still wet. Leave the paste for an hour or two until it sets hard. You can then, if you wish, paint the shells with clear varnish.

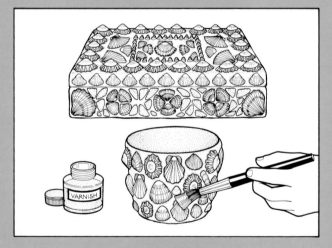

8   Study closely some of the animals that hide on rocks or in seaweed at low tide. Periwinkles, dog whelks, whelks, limpets or crabs are some of the animals you might look for. Gently put one animal at a time on to the bottom of a rock pool. Watch the animal carefully. What does it do? How does it move? Does the animal eat during the time you are watching it? What does it eat? Now try an animal of a different kind.

9   Collect interesting pebbles of different colors and shapes. Some beaches are made of smooth pebbles. The pebbles have been made smooth when they were rolled against each other by the waves.

The colors of the pebbles you have collected will show up well if you put them in a shallow dish and cover them with water. Or you can wash the pebbles in tap water, dry them, and then paint them with clear varnish. You could use some of the larger pebbles as paper weights. Display the smaller ones on a nature table or in boxes lined with cotton. Give each pebble a label that says where and when you found the pebble.

10   Imagine you find a bottle on the beach with a message inside, and write a story about it. Many people like to throw bottles with messages in them into the sea. They hope that one day a reply will come from a distant land.

Pretend that the message inside the bottle you pick up says, "Help! I am a prisoner in the old lighthouse." Describe what you do and what happens.

11 Write a poem about the seashore during a storm. Make some music to go with your poem. What instruments will you use for the wind and waves? Write your music down if you can.

12 Hatch some brine shrimp eggs. It is difficult to keep most sea animals in an aquarium. This is because they need plenty of oxygen, which they usually get when the waves stir up the water.

However, the brine shrimp is one little creature that is quite easy to keep whether you live near the sea or a long way inland.

The eggs of this tiny animal are collected from the edges of salt lakes in the United States. The eggs are sold in pet shops. They will last for years if they are kept dry and left in a fairly cool place.

Before you can hatch some brine shrimp eggs, you must first boil about ½ pint of tap water and then leave it to cool.

Tip some of the dried eggs into a wide-necked glass jar. Then add half a tablespoonful of cooking salt. Do *not* use salt from a box that has the word *iodine* or *iodized* on it. Add the cooled, boiled tap water and stir. Mark the level of the water on the outside of the jar with a piece of tape or a crayon. Leave the jar in a warm place. If the water level in the jar begins to fall, add some more tap water that has been boiled and cooled. There is no need to add any more salt.

After about 40 hours watch for the eggs to hatch. Use a magnifier to see them with.

Your brine shrimps feed on bacteria. These will grow in the water if you put a tiny piece of cabbage or lettuce leaf in it. The piece of leaf should not be any bigger than your fingernail. Put a new piece of leaf in the water when the last piece of leaf is gone.

Every few days pour the shrimps and salt water into a new clean jar. This is so that more oxygen dissolves in the water as you pour it.

13 Make a model harbor and seaside scene. Use papier mâché for the sand dunes, cliffs and rocks. Make the harbor walls from thin pieces of wood. Use small cardboard boxes for the buildings, and blue paper for the sea. Paint the tips of the waves white. You could use real sand or yellow paint for the beach. Paint the rest of your model.

Seaweed

Many kinds of seaweeds grow on the rocks and breakwaters at the seashore. Some common kinds are shown on this page.

Seaweeds are plants but they have no flowers or roots. What looks like a seaweed's root is called a holdfast. The holdfast helps the seaweed to stay firmly attached to a rock or piece of wood.

Seaweeds can be brown, red or green. The brown kinds are the most common. Bladder wrack is a common brown seaweed. It has lots of air bladders on it that help it to float. Sea lettuce looks a little like the lettuce we eat with our salads.

A seaweed that is uncovered when the tide goes out might soon dry up and die. To prevent this, seaweeds are covered with a slimy substance that does not dry up quickly. It is this slimy substance that makes seaweeds slippery to walk over. The big brown seaweeds have huge holdfasts to attach them to the rocks. They grow in deeper water and are not uncovered very often or for very long.

Seaweeds provide shelter and food for many sea animals. Some farmers put seaweeds on their fields to make the crops grow better. Seaweeds are used to make some chemicals, and foods such as ice cream, puddings and jellies. Some seaweeds can be eaten.

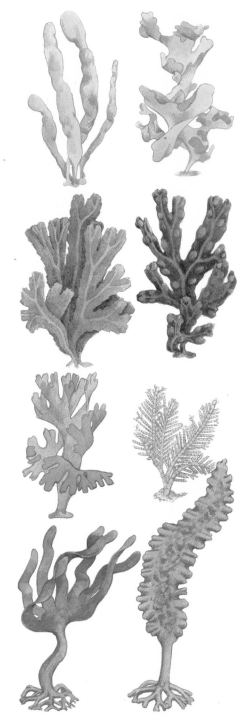

Enteromorpha
Saw wrack
Dulse
Oarweeds

Sea lettuce
Bladder wrack
Coral weed

The tidemark

Mermaids' purses

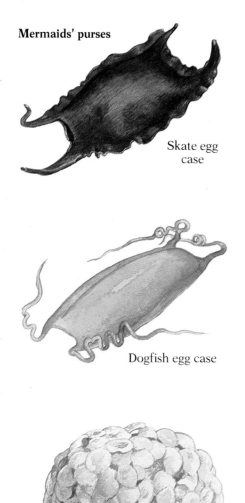

Skate egg case

Dogfish egg case

Whelk eggs

Beach flea

Sand dune with marram grass

Many things float in the sea. When the tide stops coming up the shore, these things are left. They form a line along the shore. This line is called a tidemark. You can find lots of seaweeds along the tidemark. There are pieces of wood. There is rubbish dropped from ships. Many empty sea-shells are also washed up by the tide and can be found along the beach.

Sometimes fishes' egg cases are washed ashore. The egg cases of dogfish and skates are often called mermaids' purses. The eggs hatch in deep water. Then the empty egg cases are washed ashore. The whelk is a large animal that looks like a snail. Its egg cases stick together in a spongy ball. These egg cases are often washed ashore by the tide.

Many pieces of seaweeds get broken off by the waves and washed up on the beach. If you turn over some of the seaweed on the tidemark, you may see tiny animals called beach fleas. These tiny relations of the crabs and prawns hop about all over the sand. They can burrow into the sand when they want to. Beach fleas feed on decayed seaweed and the remains of dead animals that have been washed ashore.

Sea birds

Black-headed gull

Herring gull

There are many kinds of gulls by the sea. One common kind is the black-headed gull. Its head is not black but a dark brown. Black-headed gulls have the dark head feathers only in the spring and summer. In winter their heads are almost white with just a thin dark stripe over each eye. Herring gulls are much larger than black-headed gulls. A herring gull has a red spot on its yellow beak.

The tern is very similar to a black-headed gull. It has a black cap on its head. But its tail is long and forked like that of a swallow. A tern flies out over the sea until it sees a fish. It suddenly stops and dives straight down into the water to catch the fish.

Common tern

Another bird you will often see on sandy or muddy shores when the tide is out is the oyster-catcher. This bird is black and white. Its legs are bright orange-red and its long beak is red. The oystercatcher eats large numbers of cockles and winkles, and it also digs for worms.

Oystercatcher

Sometimes you may see a large dark-colored bird. It is a cormorant. It dives underwater and stays there for about a minute catching fish. Then the cormorant stands on a rock or cliff and stretches out its wings to dry.

Cormorant

Sand dunes and shingle beaches

There are often sand dunes above the tidemark on sandy shores. These are small hills made of sand that has been blown along by the wind. Although the sand is very dry, some plants can grow in it. Marram grass and sea couch grass can grow on sand dunes. They help to stop the dunes from being blown away.

There are a number of other interesting plants that grow on sand dunes. Sea holly has prickly leaves like those of the holly tree. It has beautiful pale blue flowers. Sea sandwort has small whitish flowers and glossy yellow-green leaves. A common plant on many sand dunes is ragwort. Its yellow flowers are rather like small dandelion flowers.

Rabbits often make their burrows in the sides of sand dunes. They feed on the sand dune plants. Foxes and weasels may live on the dunes or visit them. These animals feed on the rabbits. Sometimes foxes also catch crabs and other sea creatures.

Not many plants can grow on shingle or pebble beaches. But the sea holly can grow there. So can sea kale, sea campion and the yellow-horned poppy. The plants that grow on the pebbles and shingle have very long roots. This is so they can reach the water that drains quickly through the stones.

Ragwort

Sea holly

Sea campion

Yellow-horned poppy

Sea kale

Sea sandwort

Divers and fuels

Without air we would quickly die. Divers working underwater need air to breathe. Some divers carry air tanks on their backs. Other divers who go down into the deeper parts of the sea wear special suits. They have strong diving helmets. They carry weights on their backs and chests to make them sink. A hose brings air to the diver from a pump on the ship above. Without this air the diver would not be able to breathe.

Oil drilling platform

Undersea coal mine

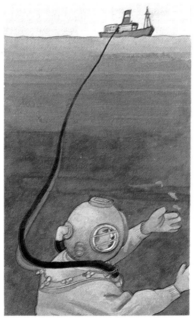

Some of our fuels come from under the sea. There is coal in some rocks under the sea. Long tunnels go out into the layers of coal from mines on the land.

In some places there is gas and oil under the sea. Floating drilling platforms are built if the sea is deep. The holes are lined with pipes as they are drilled. Big pipes or special ships carry the gas or oil to the land.

Fishing for food

Fish market

Many fish are good to eat. People go out in boats to catch them. One kind of fishing boat is called a drifter. A drifter uses long nets with corks or floats on them. The net hangs down like a curtain just below the surface of the sea. The boat and net drift along with the wind and tide. Fish swim into the net and get caught in it. Then the net and fish are pulled into the boat.

Another kind of fishing boat is called a trawler. Trawlers stay at sea for a long time. A trawler uses a net like a big string bag. The net is pulled along until it is full of fish. When the net is full, it is very heavy. So a trawler uses a big machine to pull in its nets. The fish are frozen to keep them fresh until the trawler gets back to port.

Lobster pot

Lobsters and crabs swim in the sea. Fishermen catch lobsters and crabs in special pots. You can see a lobster pot in the picture. The fisherman puts some pieces of fish in the pot. Then the pot is lowered to the bottom of the sea. If a lobster goes into the pot after a piece of fish, it cannot get out again.

Drifter   Trawler

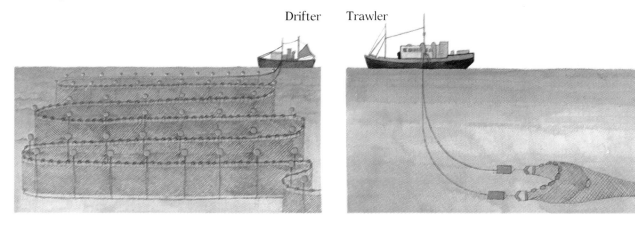

The deep sea

As we have already seen, in the deepest parts of the sea it is very dark. It is also very cold. There is no plankton in these deep waters. But there are some very strange fish. These fish that live in the black depths of the sea are themselves black, or else brown or dark purple. Because there is no plankton, these fish eat other fish.

Some of these deep-sea fish have lights on their bodies. One kind has a little light on its head. Other fish come to look at the light. Then they are caught and eaten. If an enemy comes near the deep-sea fish, the lights are turned off. Some deep-sea creatures are blind. They find their way about by means of fins and feelers.

Only a few people have ever explored the deep parts of the sea. They have taken flashlight photographs to show some of the things they have found there. We know quite a lot about the moon, which is thousands of miles away. But we know very little about the deepest parts of the sea.

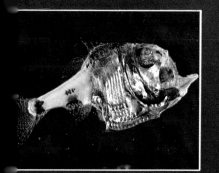
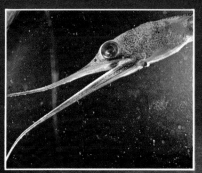

Pollution

Most of the fish we eat comes from the sea.
Many other animals and plants live near or in
the sea. But the plants and animals in the sea,
including the fish, are in great danger. So too are
the birds that live on the shore or catch their
food in the sea. The danger is from pollution.
Pollution is the dirtying of the environment.

One way in which the sea becomes polluted is
by oil. If a ship is damaged, oil from it may spill
into the sea. Oil tankers are very big. Many of
them weigh more than 200,000 tons. An oil
tanker cannot stop quickly. If one has an
accident, it can spill huge quantities of oil. Oil
from ships can dirty the beaches and kill plants
and animals. Millions of sea birds, fishes,
seaweeds, plankton and many small animals
have all died from oil pollution in recent years.

Some ships carry poisonous substances. If one
of these ships had an accident, the poison could
get into the sea. Again wildlife would be
destroyed. Poisons and trash dumped into
rivers also end up in the sea. We shall have to be
much more careful in the future how we use
the sea if we want it to stay clean and
interesting.

Oiled seabirds

Fish that have died in polluted water

Do you remember?

1 How are seaweeds different from other plants?

2 What does a seaweed's holdfast do?

3 What colors can seaweeds be?

4 Why are seaweeds covered with a slimy substance?

5 What are some of the things seaweeds are used for?

6 Name some of the things that can be found along the tidemark.

7 Where do beach fleas live?

8 When does the head of a black-headed gull have the dark feathers?

9 What is a herring gull's beak like?

10 What is a tern like?

11 What does a cormorant feed on?

12 How are sand dunes made?

13 Name some of the plants that grow on sand dunes.

14 What kind of roots have the plants that grow on shingle beaches?

15 How do divers get their air?

16 Name three fuels that can be found at the bottom of the sea.

17 What is a drifter's fishing net like?

18 How do trawlers catch fish?

19 What happens to the fish that trawlers catch?

20 How are lobsters caught?

21 Why do some deep-sea fishes have little lights on them?

22 What is pollution?

23 How can the sea become polluted?

24 What happens to the poisons and trash dumped in rivers?

Things to do

1 **Make a collection of some of the seaweeds that have been washed up by the tide.** Arrange the bigger seaweeds neatly on several sheets of newspaper. Place a few more sheets of newspaper on top of them. Put some heavy books or blocks of wood on top to weigh the paper down. Change the papers each day until the seaweeds are really dry. Paste each seaweed lightly into an exercise book or onto poster board. Label each one.

2   Find out if it is possible to use seaweed to forecast the weather. Many people say that a piece of seaweed can show you what the weather is going to be like.

Find a good-sized piece of seaweed. Take it home and hang it up in a shed, garage, greenhouse, or porch. Is the seaweed wet before the weather is rainy? Is the seaweed dry before a period of fine, dry weather?

3   Make a collection of things that have been washed up on the tidemark. Some of the things you might include in your collection are seashells, whelk egg cases, mermaids' purses, crab shells and claws, dried dead starfish, and sea urchins' shells. Wash the things you have collected in tap water. Dry them and display them on a nature table, or glue them onto poster board.

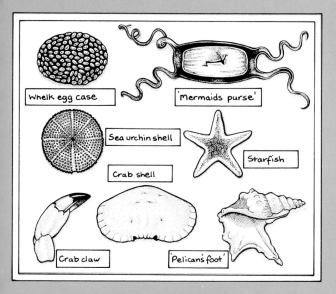

Whelk egg case
'mermaids purse'
Sea urchin shell
Starfish
Crab shell
Crab claw
'Pelican's foot'

4   Collect unusual-looking pieces of wood from the beach. There are often lots of pieces of wood washed up on the tidemark. Some of them have interesting shapes because the sea has rubbed them against the sand and shingle. Sometimes branches and pieces of roots are shaped like animals' heads.

Rub the pieces of wood smooth with sandpaper. Paint them with clear varnish.

5   Do a survey of litter you find on the beach. Walk along the tidemark with a grown-up. Look carefully at all the plastic bottles and containers that have been washed ashore. Try to tell from the labels where the litter has come from. How do you think the litter got to your particular part of the beach? Make sure that you do not handle any of the litter without checking with the grown-up.

6   Make a big picture of a fishing drifter or trawler. Ask your friends to help. Use paints, scraps of cloth, tissue paper and clear tape. Do not forget to show the nets and some of the fish the boat has caught.

7   Pretend that you are a rabbit living in a burrow on the sand dunes, and write a story about your adventures. You are going out looking for food. Think about whether you would be looking for food in the daytime or at night. What other animals might you see? Who or what would you need to hide from? What food would you be looking for? Think about how you would move, and what you would see, hear and smell. Think about how you would feel. You could make up some music to go with your story.

8   Make a book about the seashore. Write and draw what you can find out about the plants and animals in and near the sea.

Experiments to try

9 Make a collection of plaster casts of animal footprints. Look for good, clear footprints in mud or fine wet sand.

Cut a strip of poster board about 2 inches wide and bend it into a circle large enough to surround the whole footprint. Gently push the ring into the sand or mud around the footprint. Fasten the ends of the board with clear tape or a paper clip.

Put some water into an old jug, jar or bowl, and add plaster of Paris powder to it, a little at a time. Stir the mixture thoroughly. Keep adding plaster until the mixture is about as thick as molasses. Then pour the plaster gently into the circle of board you have made. Pour in enough plaster to come up to the top of the ring. While the plaster is still liquid, gently smooth the top until it is quite level. Wash out the jar, jug or bowl with water.

Leave the plaster to harden in the footprint for about 15 minutes. The whole thing can then be dug up with a trowel, wrapped up in a newspaper and taken home.

The next day, unwrap your plaster cast. Carefully take off the strip of board. Use a gentle stream of cold water from the tap to wash off the sand or mud. Use an old toothbrush or paintbrush to loosen the mud or sand from the cracks and crevices.

Leave the cast to dry. You can then paint the plaster cast if you wish, using poster paint. Paint the background a different color from the footprint. Label the plaster cast, saying what kind of animal made the footprint, where and when.

Do your experiments carefully. Write or draw what you have done and what happens. Say what you have learned. Compare your findings with those of your friends.

1 Obtaining salt from seawater

What you need: A bottle of clean seawater; a clean saucer.

What you do: Stand the saucer on a warm windowsill or over a radiator. Fill the saucer with seawater. Look at the saucer every day. What happens to the water? Look at what is left in the saucer with a hand lens or magnifying glass.

Do you now know why seas in warm countries are saltier than those in cold countries?

If you do not live near the sea, you could still make some "seawater" by adding salt to tap water. You could then do the experiment.

2 Why can people float better in the sea than in fresh water?

What you need: A jam jar or a can with the label still on it; two bowls, both the same size; some salt; some clay.

What you do: Half fill one bowl with tap water. Float the can or jar in it. If the jar or can is so light that it falls over in the water, put a little clay in the bottom.

Notice exactly how far the water comes up the outside of the can or jar when it is floating. You can see by the writing on the label how far the water comes up the outside of the can or jar.

Now fill the other bowl with tap water to exactly the same depth as the first bowl. Pour some salt into the water. Stir until the salt has all dissolved. Now float the can or jar in the salt water. Does it float higher or lower in the water? Add some more salt to the water. Stir until it all dissolves. What happens to the can or jar now?

Can you now understand why it is so easy to float and swim in the very salty Dead Sea?

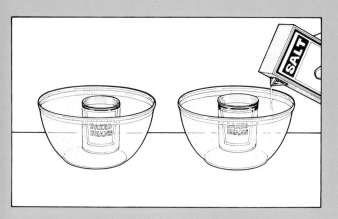

3 Why does the sea not freeze as easily as ponds and lakes?

Have you noticed that ponds, lakes and gravel pits often freeze over in cold weather? And yet it is very rare for the sea to freeze, even at the edges.

What you need: Two yogurt cups or margarine containers; some salt.

What you do: Half fill both containers with tap water. Stir three or four heaping teaspoonsfuls of salt into the water in one of the containers. Stir until the salt has all dissolved. Ask a grown-up to carefully put both containers in the freezing compartment

of a refrigerator. Look at the containers about every 30 minutes. Which container of water freezes first?

Now do the experiment again. This time fill both containers with water. Stir 3 heaping teaspoonfuls of salt into the water in one container. Stir 6 heaping teaspoonfuls of salt into the water in the other container. Which container of water freezes first?

4 Where do periwinkles and dog whelks move to?

What you need: Some pots of quick-drying enamel paints of different colors; fine paintbrushes.

What you do: Wait until the tide has started to go out. Then find some large periwinkles, dog whelks or limpets. Mark each one with a spot of paint of a different color. Mark the rock beside each animal with a spot of paint of the same color. Write down in your notebook where the marked animals are. When the tide goes out again the next day, see if you can find your marked animals. How many can you find? How far have they moved? Can you see what they have been eating?

Mark some more mollusk shells and the rocks beside them. This time carefully move the animals about 1 foot from where you found them. If you move limpets, you will have to gently lift them off the rock with the blade of a strong table knife.

Look for the animals again at low tide the next day. Have they moved at all? Have any of them gone back to the spot where you first found them?

Glossary

Here are the meanings of some words you might have met for the first time in this book.

Boulder: a very large piece of rock.

Breakwaters: walls off the shore that protect beaches or harbors from the force of waves.

Dissolve: when a substance such as sugar or salt disappears after it is placed in a liquid such as water, we say the substance dissolves.

Mollusks: a group of soft-bodied animals, many of which have a hard shell. Snails, slugs, periwinkles, whelks, cockles, mussels, limpets and razor clams are all mollusks.

Ocean: a very large sea. There are five great oceans: the Atlantic, Pacific, Indian, Arctic and Antarctic oceans.

Pebbles: small worn and rounded stones.

Plankton: the millions of tiny plants and animals that float near the surface of the sea.

Pollution: the dirtying of water (or air).

Sand dunes: small hills made of sand that has been heaped up by the wind.

Shore: the place where the land and sea meet.

Shingle: very small stones.

Tides: the rise and fall of the seawater twice each day.

Waves: the movements of water caused mainly by the wind.

Acknowledgments

The publishers would like to thank the following for permission to reproduce transparencies:

Heather Angel: p. 19; Ardea London/E Mickleburgh: p. 22; Barnaby's Picture Library: p. 26 (top right and bottom); J Allan Cash: p. 26 (top left); Bruce Coleman Ltd: J Burton p. 4 (bottom), p. 8 and cover, A Compost p. 27 (bottom right), J Dermid p. 27 (top right), N Myers p. 26 (center), R K Pilsbury p. 3 (bottom), M Richards p. 27 (bottom and top left and center right), W E Ruth p. 4 (top), T Wood p. 23; Terry Jennings: p. 21; Oxford Scientific Films: p. 3 (top), p. 5 and cover (Zig Leszczvnski c Earth Scenes), p. 6 and p. 24; ZEFA/W Braun: p. 2.

Index